Swami Vivekananda

A PATRIOT, A YOGI AND A REFORMER

Manasvi Vohra

V&S PUBLISHERS

F-2/16, Ansari Road, Daryaganj, New Delhi - 110002
☎ 23240026, 23240027 • *Fax:* 011-23240028
✉ info@vspublishers.com • 🌐 www.vspublishers.com

 **Online Brand Store: amazon.in/vspublishers**

Regional Office: Hyderabad
5-1-707/1, Brij Bhawan (Beside Central Bank of India Lane)
Bank Street, Koti, Hyderabad - 500 095
☎ 040-24737290
✉ vspublishershyd@gmail.com

Follow us on:   

BUY OUR BOOKS FROM: AMAZON FLIPKART

© Copyright: *V&S* PUBLISHERS
ISBN 978-81-978303-0-3
New Edition

DISCLAIMER

While every attempt has been made to provide accurate and timely information in this book, neither the author nor the publisher assumes any responsibility for errors, unintended omissions or commissions detected therein. The author and publisher make no representation or warranty with respect to the comprehensiveness or completeness of the contents provided.

All matters included have been simplified under professional guidance for general information only without any warranty for applicability on an individual. Any mention of an organization or a website in the book by way of citation or as a source of additional information doesn't imply the endorsement of the content either by the author or the publisher. It is possible that websites cited may have changed or removed between the time of editing and publishing the book.

Results from using the expert opinion in this book will be totally dependent on individual circumstances and factors beyond the control of the author and the publisher.

It makes sense to elicit advice from well informed sources before implementing the ideas given in the book. The reader assumes full responsibility for the consequences arising out from reading this book.

For proper guidance, it is advisable to read the book under the watchful eyes of parents/guardian. The purchaser of this book assumes all responsibility for the use of given materials and information.

The copyright of the entire content of this book rests with the author/publisher. Any infringement/ transmission of the cover design, text or illustrations, in any form, by any means, by any entity will invite legal action and be responsible for consequences thereon.

Publisher's Note

Since the beginning of our operations in 2010, **V&S Publishers** has been devoted to bringing you one of the best and widest selections of books from across reading genres. Our work is defined by our very name, Value and Substance (V&S), which is at the heart of the books we publish. In becoming one of the leading publishers of general trade books in the mass-appeal genre in India, we have focused on developing a repertoire of titles that not just seek to inspire our readers to grow and flourish in life, but also spark a love for varied cultures and languages. Today, our catalogue has expanded to more than 1000 titles, across the categories of academic, children's stories, parenting, popular science, religion and spirituality, self-improvement, and many more.

Swami Vivekananda, a towering figure in the history of modern India has left an indelible mark on the world through his teachings and life. As a proponent of yoga and Vedanta philosophy, he attempted to combine Indian spirituality with western materialism. This biography delves deep into Vivekananda's journey from his early years in Calcutta, his profound spiritual experiences with Ramakrishna, to his travels across the globe, spreading the message of self-awakening and universal brotherhood. He tirelessly worked against social evils for the upliftment of the masses. His establishment of the Ramakrishna Mission and Math continues to serve humanity to this day. His works continues to inspire millions to seek higher truths and to live a life of purpose and service.

We sincerely hope our effort in bringing out this offering will be greeted by the warm and enthusiastic reception of our readers.

Contents

Childhood and Early Life

Considered one of the greatest Indian monks, philosophers, religious teachers, and authors, Swami Vivekananda was born as Narendranath Datta in Kolkata (previously known as Calcutta) on 12th January in 1863. A disciple of the famous mystic, Shri Ramakrishna, Swami Vivekananda is credited with introducing Yoga and Vedanta to the West, spreading awareness about interfaith relations, and elevating Hinduism to the status of a world religion. Described as "an orator by Divine right and undoubtedly the greatest figure at the Parliament" by an American newspaper, Vivekananda played a crucial role in disseminating the philosophy of Hinduism across the world.

It was the day of Makar Sankranti on 12th January and millions of devotees had gathered on the banks of the River Ganges in Kolkata. Vivekananda was born at 6.33 am, just a few minutes before sunrise that day. It is interesting to note that the birth of the great philosopher coincided with city-wide prayers and celebrations by scores of men and women on the occasion of Makar Sankranti.

A Message in a Dream

Swami Vivekananda was born in an aristocratic *kayastha* Bengali family to the princely Viswanath Datta and his wife, Bhuvaneswari Datta. Although the couple already had two daughters, Bhuvaneswari Mata (as she was commonly known) expressed the desire to have a son. As was the tradition then, she prayed, fasted, and followed all religious customs so that she is blessed with a boy.

(a) Mother of Swami Vivekananda: *(b) Brother of Swami Vivekananda*
Bhuvaneswari Datta

One day, she requested a relative who used to live in Varanasi, in Uttar Pradesh, to offer special prayers for her to Lord Shiva so that she may conceive a son. Following this event, Bhuvaneswari Mata had a dream one night in which Lord Shiva appeared to her and told her he would be born as her son. The next day, she woke up extremely happy with her dream.

Soon, a child was born to the aristocratic couple and was named Vireswara by Bhuvaneswari Mata. Later, however, the family named the child Narendranath Datta, lovingly shortened to "Naren" by the family members.

Family Roots

The Datta family was among the prominent families in 19th-century Calcutta, known for their influence, affluence, pioneering ideas, and philanthropic work. Known for his erudite personality, Viswanath Datta served as an attorney in the High Court of Calcutta. He was well-versed in English and

Persian works and was fond of quoting from Hafiz's works, which he believed to contain wisdom unlike any other.

<table>
<tr><td>

What's in a Name?

Swami Vivekananda's family members wanted to name him "Durgadas". But he was named "Veereshwar" – which was his name at home – owing to the dream that Bhuvaneswari had before he was born. He was officially named Narendranath.

</td></tr>
</table>

Viswanath's father, Durgacharan, had already renounced worldly life in search of spirituality after his first son was born. Unlike his father, Viswanath was much into worldly affairs: he enjoyed cooking treating his friends to banquets, and travelling to places of interest. A non-believer when it came to social conventions of the time, he was a kind-hearted man who often went out of his way to help people in need. Viswanath was also a strict disciplinarian and ensured his children were always at their best behaviour.

Swami Vivekananda's mother, Bhuvaneswari Devi, was a traditional Hindu in her beliefs. Stately in her appearance and courteous in her conduct, she spent her time managing the household, reading Hindu epics, singing, and sewing. She went on to dedicate her life to help the needy and spent her life in service to the Divine. Bhuvaneswari Devi and Viswanath had two sons – besides young Vivekananda – and four daughters, two of whom passed away at a young age.

A Brush with Spirituality

Young Vivekananda was a sweet but restless child. A ball of energy, he would run around the house, playing, teasing his sisters. Sometimes, his mother would put his head under a tap dispensing cold water and pray to Lord Shiva, to calm his senses. An animal lover, young Vivekananda had a cow, a goat, a monkey, a few pigeons, guinea pigs, and even a peacock as pets to keep him company. With his striking resemblance to his grandfather, many people in the family believed him to be his reincarnation.

Bhuvaneswari Devi taught Bangla and the alphabets of the English language to young Vivekananda. She would also read him stories from the *Ramayana* and *Mahabharata*. Even at a young age, Vivekananda showed great devotion to Hindu deities – he created his own little space with idols of Lord Rama and his consort, Sita, decorated with flowers. Later, he replaced their idols with that of Lord Shiva as he was regarded as the God of Renunciation. Notwithstanding the change in his view, he deeply revered the *Ramayana*.

Early Days as a Student

Young Vivekananda started attending primary school at the age of six years. In the company of his classmates, Vivekananda had learned some objectionable words. His parents overheard him when he used such words at home. His parents were deeply disappointed at his behaviour, and this led them to withdraw him from school and engage a private tutor for him at home. Soon after, young Vivekananda demonstrated sharp cognitive skills and a strong memory. He was could easily memorise long passages from the epics *Mahabharata* and *Ramayana* and was exceptional at Sanskrit. During this time, he met some of his friends, who went on to be his friends, throughout his life and always stood beside him.

King and Court
Young Vivekananda was fond of playing the game of "King and the Court". He would always play the role of the King and his friends would play ministers and state officials. It is interesting to note that his name Narendra (which means "Lord of Men") indicated that he was destined to be a leader of men from birth.

Vivekananda's personality was largely shaped by the thoughts and beliefs of his parents. Hence, since early childhood, he believed in equality. He felt no human should be considered superior to another.

By the time, Vivekananda turned eight years old, he again started attending school. He demonstrated his ability at academics soon after he joined the school. His teachers and classmates acknowledged his efforts to perform well in the academics. This was also when he was introduced to the English language, which he was a bit reluctant to study at first owing to its foreign nature. But when he took it up, he learnt it with great dedication.

Young Vivekananda played many games and even invented many of his own. He was trained in various sports, including wrestling, fencing, and rowing. Additionally, he established a gymnasium and an amateur theatre company. He even tried to learn to cook at a young age. His childhood restlessness enabled him to explore many co-curricular activities and develop new hobbies. Deep down, he believed that he would become a monk someday.

Swami Vivekananda playing with his friends

2

Education and Initial Spiritual Enlightenment

In 1877, Swami Vivekananda and his family moved to Raipur. While his family was travelling to Raipur in the Central Province, young Vivekananda – who was 15 years old then – experienced spiritual ecstasy for the first time. The family was aboard a bullock cart and was passing through a scenic stretch shaded with trees and full of colourful flowerbeds. As the bullock cart trudged along a treacherous path, with cliffs rising on both sides, Vivekananda

Swami Vivekananda in his youth

spotted a bee hive nestled in a cliff crevice. The sight of the bee hive filled him with admiration for all life created by the Divine. At this point, he lost consciousness and lay limp as the cart made its way. Even when he regained his consciousness, he continued to be in a state of spiritual ecstasy over what he had realised.

This initial brush with spiritual enlightenment came against a backdrop of young Vivekananda, who underwent a shift in his temperament. As he grew into an adolescent, he started showing a keen understanding of intellectual matters of concern. This was accompanied by his appetite for consuming information, whether in the form of books specialising in history and literature, or newspapers. He also grew interested in music during this time, believing it should represent high ideals of a musician.

Education During Adolescent Years

In Raipur, Vivekananda's father encouraged him to spend time in the company of scholars of the time. His family supported his interactions and deep-diving into intellectual topics of interest. During these discussions, Vivekananda showed great intellect and a prodigious memory. He displayed the comprehension of truth in its most profound form and from various perspectives.

A New Way of Reading a Book

Young Vivekananda developed a new way of reading a book and its subject matter without reading the pages line-by-line. He would read the opening and closing sentences of a page to understand the subject. This enabled him to understand the overall trend of the argument presented by an author by reading just a few lines. One could say Swami Vivekananda was among the pioneers of "speed reading".

Swami Vivekananda was considered as one of the pioneers of speed-reading

In 1879, Vivekananda and his family returned to Calcutta from Raipur. In Calcutta, he was enrolled in Presidency College, where he scored a first division in the entrance examination. During these years, Vivekananda developed a well-rounded taste in literature, with his interests primarily resting in English and Bengali literature. His favourite subjects were history, philosophy, religion, science, and art. He also took a keen interest in Hindu scriptures, notably the *Vedas*, *Upanishad*, and the *Bhagavad Gita*, as well as the epics of *Ramayana* and *Mahabharata*.

Swami Vivekananda was interested
in not only academic subjects but also Hindu Scriptures

In 1880, Vivekananda entered the General Assembly's Institution, which the Scottish General Missionary Board established. Later, it came to be known as the Scottish Church College. Here, he studied Western philosophy, Western logic, and European history. By 1884, he obtained his Bachelor of Arts degree. During this time, he familiarised himself with the works of Immanuel Kant, Baruch Spinoza, David Hume, Georg W.F. Hegel, August Comte, and John Stuart Mill.

He developed a fascination for the concept of evolutionism as propounded by Herbert Spencer. Over time, he went on to translate Spencer's book *Education* (1861) into Bangla. During his examination days, he would often stay up through the night to study by subsisting on tea or coffee.

Brushes with Spiritual Enlightenment

While Vivekananda was studying at Scottish Church College, the principal of the college, William Hastie – Professor of English Literature – introduced him to Shri Ramakrishna. Hastie viewed Vivekananda as a genius. Additionally, he felt that he had never come across a student with the kind of potential that the young man had shown in academics and intellectual thought.

The Night Before

A day before Vivekananda's B.A examination, he was suddenly consumed by love for the Divine and suddenly broke into a song, praising nature as a Divine Creation. His friends urged him to study for the exam the day. However, Vivekananda continued – at the throes of beginning his monastic life. He wrote the exam the next day and passed it with flying colours.

The meeting with Shri Ramakrishna marked a turning point in Vivekananda's life. This association went on to trigger a spiritual awakening in the young man. With time, he started believing that everything in this world is temporary. He even questioned the utility of an academic education.

But before coming face to face with Shri Ramakrishna, Vivekananda experienced his initial brushes with spiritual enlightenment. He joined Nava Vidhan in 1880, founded by Keshab Chandra Sen. By 1884, he also became a member of the Freemasonry Lodge. During this period, he was also part of Band of Hope – also organised by Sen – which worked towards dissuading youths from taking to smoking and drinking.

Soon, it was time for Vivekananda to get married as was the tradition back then. An alliance arrived from a wealthy family for the young man. The family offered to pay for his higher studies in England, so that he could apply for the prestigious Indian Civil Service examination. However, Vivekananda refused the alliance, owing to his ideals of purity and abstinence from physical pleasures. He believed himself to be a *brahmachari* (a celibate belonging to the Hindu tradition) and turned his back on living the life of a householder. To him, keeping his soul pure was a necessary pre-condition for experiencing spiritual enlightenment. It was necessary for harnessing the power of memory, concentration, insight, and maintaining physical fitness.

Joining the Brahmo Samaj

However, it was when he joined Brahmo Samaj that Vivekananda underwent yet another major shift. Founded by Raja Rammohan Roy, it was a liberal movement that was against rituals, idol worship, and the supremacy of *brahmins* or priests in orthodox Hinduism. Instead, it focused on dedicating oneself to the worship of the "Eternal, Immutable Being" who they deemed to be the Creator of the Universe. A reformist movement, it also rallied for the emancipation of women, widow remarriage, and the abolition of child marriage, and encouraged mass education.

The Brahmo Samaj Movement struck a chord with the English-educated youths of Bengal. After Raja Rammohan Roy, the movement was led by Debendranath Tagore and Keshab Chandra Sen. The progressive ideas of the movement found appeal with Vivekananda; however, the young man continued to feel a certain sense of spiritual yearning – a void that couldn't be filled by the ideas preached by Brahmo Samaj. When he expressed his dissatisfaction about the void within to realise God to Debendranath Tagore, he instructed

Vivekananda to spend time in meditation, recognising the makings of a *yogi* within him.

Vivekananda's quest to find God led him back to William Hastie's words during one of his lectures on the poem *Excursion* by William Wordsworth. He remembered his professor having spoken about Shri Ramakrishna as being the only person who had experienced religious ecstasy as experiencing this phenomenon required great concentration and purity of soul. This marked the great turn that was now to come in Swami Vivekananda's life.

Swami Vivekananda in meditative state

3

A Fateful Meeting with Shri Ramakrishna

The fateful meeting between Shri Ramakrishna and young Vivekananda happened sometime in 1881. Inspired by his professor William Hastie's words of praise about Shri Ramakrishna, Vivekananda, decided to visit him along with his friends. At the time, he was studying hard for his impending F.A. examination. Notwithstanding the pressure of studies and examination, the young man made his way to Surendra Nath Mitra's house, where Ramakrishna was invited to deliver an address. His relative Ram Chandra Datta – who was also Vivekananda's close friend – accompanied him to Surendra Nath Mitra's house.

The Meeting Unfolds

The first meeting between Shri Ramakrishna and Vivekananda was a significant in the lives of both spiritual masters. Ramakrishna acknowledged the young boy's spiritual essence in a moment. Despite not being dressed in any finery or being the best groomed, Ramakrishna gauged his meditative state of mind and asked the young man to sing. And so young Vivekananda closed his eyes and sang the sweetest melodies that at once touched a chord with Shri Ramakrishna.

Shri Ramakrishna Paramhansa: Guru of Swami Vivekananda

After he finished singing, Ramakrishna caught young Vivekananda by his arm and led him to the porch. Vivekananda saw tears streaming down Ramakrishna's eyes as he spoke fervently and addressed him as the divine incarnation of Lord Narayana. At first, Vivekananda couldn't understand what the spiritual master was saying – the rationalist within him couldn't believe any of it. Shri Ramakrishna was so overjoyed in the moment of his spiritual realisation that he even him sweets with his hands – much like making an offering to a deity. Surprisingly, his actions dispirited young Vivekananda as it was not what he was expecting. However, he still gave him word that he would return to visit him at Dakshineswar.

Shri Ramakrishna's Vision

During one of Vivekananda's visits to Dakshineswar, Shri Ramakrishna asked him key questions to do with his birth, his past and present life, as well as his mission in the world. Young Vivekananda responded to these questions in a state of stupor. Ramakrishna was so moved by his responses that he declared Vivekananda to be one of the legendary Seven Sages who reside in the realm of Gods and Ascended Masters.

A sketch showing interaction between
Swami Vivekananda and Ramakrishna near a river

Young Vivekananda visited Shri Ramakrishna in Dakshineswar the following year with his friends. The initial interactions with Ramakrishna were somewhat riddled with conflict, owing to Vivekananda's inability to accept the spiritual guru's behaviour towards him. Initially, he saw Ramakrishna's utterances and his vision of him as delusional. His initial visits to Dakshineswar were eventful with Vivekananda almost believing he was under a hypnotic spell of the former. These events almost made the young man think that Ramakrishna was a madman. Yet, he couldn't deny the spiritual attraction he felt towards him.

The Spiritual Guru and his Disciple

Shri Ramakrishna, on the other hand, was nothing short of besotted with his new disciple. Young Vivekananda continued to rebel against his ideas. Being a member of the Brahmo Samaj, he was against polytheism, and Ramakrishna, on the other hand, worshipped the idol of Goddess Kali. He also took an oppositional stance towards the *Advaita Vedanta* which outlined "the identity with the absolute". However, Shri Ramakrishna handled all his arguments against his ideas with utmost patience and even a degree of the reverence. Often, he would tell his young disciple *"... to see truth from all angles ... "*.

Young Vivekananda spent five years studying Shri Ramakrishna at Dakshineswar is rational-critical self never allowed him to believe blindly in the words of Ramakrishna, and the latter appreciated that. Such was the story of a rather stubborn disciple and a patient, ever-forgiving teacher who encouraged his student to question everything. Ramakrishna's approach to Vivekananda's infinite curiosity and inclination for reasoning enabled him to train his disciple's mind and tame his spirit to nurture a spiritual discipline, which was essential for leading a spiritual life.

However, this also led to feelings of envy among other students at Dakshineswar. Ramakrishna would never listen to any criticism against Vivekananda, because of the love he felt in his soul towards the young man, believing him to be an incarnation of Lord Narayana. However, with time, due to studies, Vivekananda couldn't make it to Dakshineswar nearly as often. Naren's absence, disappointed Ramakrishna – sometimes he was so overcome with sadness at his prolonged absence that he would visit Calcutta or send someone to bring him to Dakshineswar.

A Master's Love for his Disciple

Once Ramakrishna himself travelled to Calcutta to see Vivekananda, who'd not been able to visit him for some time. Vivekananda was singing a prayer at the Brahmo temple when his spiritual guru entered the place. Hearing his voice, Ramakrishna slipped into a religious ecstasy and a commotion followed. When the young disciple reprimanded him, Ramakrishna became teary eyed and told him he couldn't bear Vivekananda's absence any longer.

The Change of Tide

In 1884, Vivekananda suffered a huge personal loss with his father's untimely death. This led the family to face bankruptcy with creditors lining their door for the repayment of loans. Vivekananda's fortunes had changed overnight. This family's poor economic conditions forced him to look for work to support his mother and siblings. He would often turn down invitations from his friends for lunch or dinner, thinking about his family's plight back home. By the same token, he would often skip his meals at home, saying that he'd eaten at a friend's place, so that others could receive a larger share of food.

Vivekananda and his family found themselves steeped in poverty in those years. Although he had rich friends, no one came forward to help. He spent his days roaming streets of Calcutta but he couldn't find any job that suited his skills. At this point, he found himself questioning the existence of the Divine. He now started visiting Dakshineswar more often to find solace in his troubled condition.

In time, Vivekananda found a small-time job that paid him enough to help the family with daily expenses. One day, he asked Ramakrishna to pray to Goddess Kali to deliver them from poverty and hardship. To this, Shri Ramakrishna asked him why he didn't pray to her himself. He then advised his disciple to head to her shrine, lie prostrate before her idol, pray to her earnestly, and ask for a boon – and that the boon would be granted.

This time, Vivekananda took his advice and went to the temple thrice to pray to the Goddess, but each time he forgot to pray for money. When he related the incidents to Shri Ramakrishna, the latter told him that it was not for Vivekananda to lead a worldly life and that he was created for a higher path. With that, he also assured him that his family will be able to live a simple but comfortable life.

This incident left an indelible impact on young Vivekananda. It changed his perception about God as a Supreme Being – in that he ultimately understood the idea of realising God. It brought about a shift within him spiritually and he finally accepted Shri Ramakrishna as his spiritual teacher. Vivekananda went on to spend another six years under the mentorship of Shri Ramakrishna. During this time, he underwent deep spiritual awakening that enriched his spiritual life and prepared him for the Mission in this world, which Ramakrishna always believed Vivekananda had taken birth for.

4

Establishing the Ramakrishna Math and Travels in India

In the years that followed, Vivekananda overcame material and spiritual hardships with the mentorship he received from Shri Ramakrishna. During these years, he began to experience deep empathy towards the people in need. Shri Ramakrishna – who had already received visions of Vivekananda's future self as an ascetic – often remarked that the purpose of his life was to serve humanity.

Under Shri Ramakrishna's mentorship, Vivekananda re-learned the ideals of Hinduism. The most significant shift he experienced was to see religion beyond the dogmas of society and discrimination based on of caste and creed. Ramakrishna helped him to inculcate a deep, inclusive sense of understanding towards Hinduism.

The Demise of Shri Ramakrishna

It was in 1885 that thunder struck Vivekananda yet again. For days, Shri Ramakrishna had been complaining of a throat problem. He was later diagnosed with cancer. Notwithstanding his illness, Shri Ramakrishna continued to hold classes for his disciples and this led his illness to grow worse with time. He was moved to a house in northern Calcutta and, later, to a garden house in Cossipore, a suburban area. He was looked after by Vivekananda and his other disciples who gave up on their studies and household life to take care of him.

Shri Ramakrishna continued to mentor and educate Vivekananda till his last breath. During this time, he gave away ochre-coloured robes to Vivekananda and some other disciples which marked the nascent stages of the formation of a new monastic order. In his last days, Shri Ramakrishna taught Vivekananda to always serve the mankind on behalf of the Divine and to care for other members of the monastic order. He declared Vivekananda as the monastic order's leader and asked other disciples to revere him as their leader. Shri Ramakrishna breathed his last on 16th August, 1886, in Cossipore.

The Unfinished Book of Poems
In 1887, Swami Vivekananda and Vaishnav Charan Basak put together a collection of Bengali songs, called *Sangeet Kalpataru*. While most of the songs in this compilation were collected and organised by Vivekananda, he was unable to finish his work on the book owing to certain unfavourable circumstances.

As Vivekananda assumed the role of a leader, there were certain aspects that he wanted to improve about their spiritual discipline. He would tell them repeatedly that spirituality was not just about slipping into a trance but about following the path of renunciation and acknowledging one's higher self. Those who would often slip into a trance to put on a show rather than realising spiritual goals were often prescribed medical treatment and a nourishing diet by Vivekananda! The young spiritual master placed credence on inculcating thoughts of high self-control, renouncing worldly pleasures and attachments, and developing a yearning for the Divine.

Swami Vivekananda guiding his disciples

Establishing the Ramakrishna Math

With the death of Shri Ramakrishna, new troubles dawned on Vivekananda and his devotees. With months of rent unpaid, the spiritual master and his devotees had to start looking for a new place to live. Many devotees chose to return home, leaving the monastic life in favour of living the life of a householder. Fortunately, these problems were short-lived.

One of the householder disciples of Shri Ramakrisha, Surendranath Mitra, came to their rescue and offered to pay the rent for the new place. Soon, Vivekananda found a broken-down house in Baranagore – near their earlier centre at Dakshineswar – where he decided to establish a *math* (monastery) along with his remaining disciples. This *math* marked the founding of the first Ramakrishna Math, which would become one of the most famous monastic orders in the world. The new place had a shrine room. At its center was a copper vessel containing Shri Ramakrishna's ashes. This copper vessel was daily worshipped by Vivekananda and his disciples.

At the Baranagore Math, Swami Vivekananda and his disciples lived an ascetic routine that only comprised meditation, studies, worship, and devotional music. Sometimes they would go without food and spend the whole day and night in meditation. Resources were scarce, so their meals sometimes only consisted of boiled rice, herbs, and salt.

At the math, Vivekananda continued his inward spiritual journey and undertook the spiritual education of his disciples. However, he did not want their spiritual enlightenment to be only based on embracing asceticism. Vivekananda believed that it was necessary for them to learn about the philosophical systems of the world along with spirituality. As a result, he devoted time to studying the histories of various countries and philosophies and teachings of Aristotle, Plato, Kant, Hegel, as well as of Gautama Buddha, Madhava, Ramanuja, and Chaitanya. He reconciled the similarities and differences of these systems with the teachings of Shri Ramakrishna. His disciples would also often play devotional music, which was received as a welcome change from teaching and learning.

Swami Vivekananda reading various philosophers

In the month of December in 1886, Vivekananda and eight of his disciples were invited to the village of Antpur. The monks accepted the invitation and made their way to the village. Here, on Christmas eve, Vivekananda and his disciples formally took monastic vows. On this day, Vivekananda came to be known as "Swami Vivekananda".

Setting Off on a Journey Around India

With time, the youth at the Baranagore Math grew restless and wanted to travel beyond the confines of the headquarters to various sacred spots in the country to enrich their spiritual life. Swami Vivekananda also wanted to live a life of solitude and explore his inner self and test his strength of spirituality. In 1888, he set out to explore life as a *Parivrajaka* (a wandering monk in Hindu religious philosophy) beyond the *math* and this experience changed his life forever.

Swami Vivekananda travelling around India

Armed with just a *kamandalu* (a pot for carrying water), the *Bhagavad Gita* and *The Imitation of Christ*, as well as his staff, Swami Vivekananda embarked on a transformative journey around India for five years. His first stop was Varanasi, where he met renowned Sanskrit scholar, Pramadadas Mitra. Their the mutual admiration and respect were palpable and they continued to express this in person, and later, through letters. Next, he visited Ayodhya, the birth place of Lord Rama; Lucknow, where he explored monuments and gardens from the time of the Islamic rule; Agra, where the sheer glory of Taj Mahal moved him to tears of joy; and, finally, Vrindavan, where he learned about the life of Lord Krishna.

In Hathras, Swami Vivekananda had an interesting experience. At the station, he met the station master, Sarat Chandra Gupta, with whom he established a connection instantaneously. Sarat Chandra would discuss the doctrine of Hinduism with people at the station and even entertain them with devotional music. After spending a few days with Swami Vivekananda, Sarat Chandra decided to renounce his worldly life and accompany the spiritual master to Hardwar. From Hardwar, the duo travelled onward to Hrishikesh.

The Maharaja of Alwar
When Swami Vivekananda visited Alwar, he had an audience with the Maharaja. When the Maharaja asked him why a strong young man like him was leading the life of a vagabond, Swami Vivekananda asked the Maharaja why he spent so much of his time with Westerners and went out hunting while neglecting his duty towards his people. When the Maharaja answered that it was because he enjoyed doing these activities, Swami Vivekananda retorted that like the Maharaja, he also liked to walk around as a monk.

Throughout Swami Vivekananda's travels, he came across numerous strangers whose life he touched and then those who touched his to proper him further into spiritual enlightenment. Swami Vivekananda travelled to Delhi, Jaipur, Kathiawar (in Gujarat), Baroda, Poona, Bombay, Kolhapur, Belgaum, Bangalore, Trivandrum, and Rameshwaram during his travels.

He acquainted himself with various religious traditions, visiting places of worship belonging to different faiths, and observing social structures and patterns. During his travels, he mixed around with people from all walks of life and across social strata: royalty, government officials, scholars, *dewans*, and workers belonging to the lower castes. On 31st May 1893, Swami Vivekananda left for Chicago from Bombay.

5

Travels to the West

When Swami Vivekananda reached Kanyakumari, he sat on a rock in the southernmost tip of India, and he is said to have experienced a flash in his mind of the American continent. In his perspective, America was a land of plenty of opportunities, wealth, and optimism, owing to the fact that the land was free from the restraints of caste and class. This got him thinking about taking his mission to America. He saw this as an opportunity to not just improve India's image in the West, but also to inspire Indians to expand their vision of the West. At this point, he remembered his friends – especially his friends in Kathiawar – who encouraged him to consider representing India at the Parliament of Religions in Chicago.

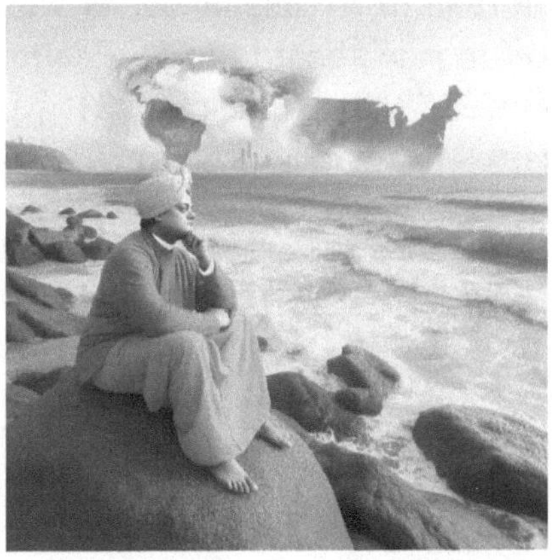

American continent which flashed across Swami Vivekananda's mind

Shri Ramakrishna Appears in a Dream

In the days when Swami Vivekananda was thinking about his trip to the United States, he had a strange dream. He saw Shri Ramakrishna walking on what seemed like an ocean and asked Vivekananda to follow him. At the same time he received a letter from Sarada Devi to whom he'd written for advice on the trip abroad. She advised him to travel to America as well. Swami Vivekananda took both the events as signs from the Divine and decided to travel to the United States.

Later, when Swami Vivekananda was in Madras, he held discussions on religion, science, philosophy, history and literature. It was also here that he publicly announced his plans to visit America. At once, his devotees started collecting funds for the trip. However, when his devotees brought him the money, he asked them to distribute it among the poor, because he thought he was getting driven by his ambition. He prayed to the Divine for guidance.

Aboard the Ship to the West

Swami Vivekananda reached Bombay along with the Raja of Khetri. The Raja gifted the iconic orange silk robes and an ochre-coloured turban to Vivekananda, as well as a purse and a first-class ticket to ride aboard the *SS Peninsular* that was to start its journey on 31st May. And so, on 31st May 1893, Swami Vivekananda started his landmark journey towards the West.

Taking Vedanta Philosophy to the West

Swami Vivekananda was responsible for introducing Vedanta philosophy to the West. His efforts also fundamentally reformed Hinduism in a big way.

It took him some time to get used to life aboard the ship, considering he had spent so much time living as a wandering monk. Initially, he would feel irritable when it came to taking care of his belongings. His robes also aroused curiosity among his co-passengers, and soon he became a popular figure onboard for his deep nature and incisive mind. The journey took him to Colombo, where he visited Hinayana Buddhist monasteries; Singapore, where he visited the hangout spots of Malay pirates; and Hong Kong, where he was delighted to observe Chinese babies strapped to the backs of their mothers as they went about their daily tasks with remarkable agility.

Then the boat finally reached Japan. Here, Swami Vivekananda visited the cities of Tokyo, Osaka, Kyoto, and Yokohama where he was intrigued to see the beautiful landscape of hills, garden-front houses, pools, and small bridges. Throughout his travels, his motherland remained in his thoughts and he often wondered about the possibility of more and more men expanding their horizons to alleviate society from extant social evils. Soon, the boat arrived in Vancouver, in British Columbia. From here, Swami Vivekananda took the train to Chicago on 30th July. This was where the Parliament of Religions had to take place.

Swami Viekananda's visit to Japan

Upon Reaching Chicago

However, to his disappointment, he found that the event had been postponed to the first week of September. He was also told that the event organisers weren't going to accept any speaker without relevant credentials awarded by an organisation of repute and would instead only be acknowledged as a delegate. All this came as a surprise to him – he hadn't brought any such letter of authority with him.

With his money dwindling, Swami Vivekananda found himself in a fix. Someone in Chicago suggest him to head to Boston where the rentals were low. During his time in Boston, he came across many people who expressed curiosity about his robes and asked strange questions about Hinduism. But there were also people who wanted to learn more about Hinduism. One such person was Professor J.H. Wright in Boston, who taught Greek at the Harvard University.

Professor Wright played an important role in inspiring Swami Vivekananda to represent Hinduism at the Parliament of Religions. He also helped him with the credentials by writing to people connected with the Parliament and even the committee chairman. He also bought Vivekananda a train ticket to Chicago. However, when he reached Chicago, he found that he'd misplaced the address of the Committee! Luckily, a society woman named Mrs. George W. Hale came to his rescue and took him to the office of the Parliament of Religions. There, Swami Vivekananda met Dr. J.H. Barrows, the President of the Parliament and a friend of Mrs. Hale. Thereon, he was readily accepted as a delegate representing Hinduism and was provided accommodation with Mr. and Mrs. John B. Lyons.

Representing India at the Parliament of Religions

The Parliament of Religions was organised upon the initiative of the Swedenborgian layman and the then judge presiding over the Illinois Supreme Court, Charles C. Bonney. The event was held along with the World's Columbian Exposition, which was organised to celebrate the 400th anniversary of the discovery of America by famous explorer Christopher Columbus. The aim was to organise a congress of people representing all the religions worldwide, and highlight the unity of religions. This congress brought together the Eastern and Western religious and spiritual thought on the world stage. Here, at the Parliament of Religions, Hinduism was represented by the Brahmo Samaj and Theosophical Society of India.

The event was opened to the audience at 10.00 am. Besides Christianity, the Parliament had represented all significant non-Christian religions, including Hinduism, Islam, Buddhism, Jainism, and Confucianism. There were around 7,000 people in attendance, watching the proceedings with intent as all the official delegates walked in, in a grand procession. Here, among the Oriental delegates sat Swami Vivekananda, as a representative of the Universal Religion of the Vedas.

Speakers at World Parliament of Religions 1893, Chicago

Oriental Delegates at the Parliament of Religions

The Parliament of Religions was attended by Pratap Chandra Mazoomdar on behalf of the Calcutta Brahmo Samaj and Nagarkar (Bombay); Gandhi representing Jainism; Dharmapala, the Ceylon Buddhists; Annie Besant and Chakravarti, the Theosophical Society; and Swami Vivekananda, the Universal Religion of the Vedas.

When it was Swami Vivekananda's turn to address the gathering, he got up and bowed to Goddess Saraswati and then began his speech. He opened the speech with "Sisters and Brothers of America" – this address alone led to a thunderous two-minute standing ovation from the audience. When it ended, Swami Vivekananda resumed his speech, quoting from the *Shiva Mahimna Strotam*:

"As the different streams having their sources in different places all mingle their water in the sea, so, O Lord, the different paths which men take, through different tendencies, various though they appear, crooked or straight, all lead to Thee!"

and,

"Whosoever comes to Me, through whatsoever form, I reach him; all men are struggling through paths that in the end lead to Me."

He concluded the speech with the need for ending bigotry, fanaticism, and sectarianism. The audience, yet again, erupted into a thunderous applause at his short but extremely meaningful speech that preached religious harmony as the ultimate truth of all faiths. The speech by Swami Vivekananda was widely reported in the American media of the time, which called him a "cyclonic monk from India". Notably, the *New York Herald* and *Boston Evening Transcript* described him as the "greatest figure in the Parliament...".

Following the congress, Swami Vivekananda spoke at various other occasions, at receptions, in private homes, and also at scientific sections. Everywhere, his speeches carried the message of religious tolerance, with emphasis on universality.

6

Teachings and Philosophy

After representing India at the Parliament of Religions, Swami Vivekananda took off on a tour of the United States. During the tour, he spent most of his time in the central and eastern parts of the US, mostly in Boston, Detroit, Chicago, and New York. He delivered lectures at various places, often ignoring his health as he went about his busy life. During this time, he also founded the Vedanta Society of New York in 1894.

But when the lecture tours began to tell on his health, he started offering private classes in Vedanta philosophy and yoga. One of his landmark lecture classes was in June 1895, when his followers congregated at Thousand Island Park, in New York, where he lectured them for two months. That said, it is not that Swami Vivekananda didn't face opposition in the United States.

American Women

Swami Vivekananda maintained an especially positive outlook towards American women. He described them as "… independent, self-relying, and kind-hearted" in his letters to his disciples and followers back in India. In yet another letter to the Maharaja of Khetri, he described how they helped him in times of need by offering him money, food, and shelter, as well as treating him as their own son or brother. In another letter, he likened them to Goddess Lakshmi and Saraswati for their beauty and learning, respectively.

While it was a country free of the dogma associated with caste as in case of India, he still faced opposition from certain "free-thinkers", atheists, rationalists, and materialists – basically people who opposed the idea of a Divine Being. In one such meeting, in New York, where he was invited by followers of Western science and philosophy, he countered their claims by demonstrating how some of the deepest questions about life and being couldn't be answered by scientific laws and principles because these things were beyond pure logic or reason and limitations posed by science. It was enough to inspire numerous people from the meeting to attend his lecture on religion the very next day!

In an interesting turn of events, Swami Vivekananda caught the interest of famous scientist Nikola Tesla who worked in the field of electricity. Tesla was impressed with Vivekananda's interpretation of the Samkhya cosmogony and the idea of cycles in Hinduism. He immediately drew a parallel with the concepts of matter and energy in Physics. Besides Tesla, other eminent scientists of the time, Professor Helmholtz and Lord Kelvin, also met him to discuss ideas.

Rejecting University Appointments

Swami Vivekananda turned down two academic positions at prestigious American institutions: the chair in Eastern Philosophy at Harvard University and a position of a similar nature at Columbia University. This was because he felt that these positions would have interfered with his duties as a monk.

As Swami Vivekananda's popularity grew in the United States, more opportunities came to him to take his teachings far and wide. He was given land southeast of San Jose, in California, where we set up a retreat for students of Vedanta Philosophy and called it *Shanti Ashrama* (Peace Retreat).

However, the largest centre of Vedanta in America continues to Vedanta Society of Southern California, in Hollywood, which is among the 12 main centres.

Throughout his tour in the US, Swami Vivekananda made sure to write back to his devotees in India about his observations in the United States. His observations mostly centred on education and the importance of hygiene. He was also passionate about working towards the emancipation of women in India. Swami Vivekananda also sent back money which he earned from his lectures to his devotees in India for religious and philanthropic work. They would often raise concern about the propaganda in the Western media about him and his teachings, but he would assure them that his Divine Mission was what was more important.

Swami Vivekananda writing letter to his followers in India

Lecture Tours in the United Kingdom

In 1895 and 1896, Swami Vivekananda visited the United Kingdom, addressing various groups of people there as well. One of the landmark moments was in 1895 when he met an Irish woman named Margaret Elizabeth Noble. His teachings made such an impact on her that she went on to become her disciple and came to be known as Sister Nivedita. She later followed Swami Vivekananda to India and is remembered for her great work as a teacher, school founder, an author, and an activist as she worked for the education of Indian women.

Margaret Elizabeth Noble (Sister Nivedita), disciple of Swami Vivekananda

Another highlight of his tour to the UK was his meeting with the famous Sanskritist and Indologist, Max Müller, in Oxford University. Max Müller had been following Shri Ramakrishna's and Keshab Chandra Sen's work for years. He'd even written article about Ramakrishna, titled "A Real Mahatman". So, it was natural for him to want to meet Swami Vivekananda. The two legendary personalities met over lunch in Oxford on 28th May 1896. Later, he also met Paul Deussen, a noted Indologist in Germany.

Followers in the West

Among the notable followers that Swami Vivekananda attracted in the United States and Europe were Lord Kelvin, Harriet Monroe, Ella Wheeler Wilcox, Robert G. Ingersoll, Sarah Bernhardt, Nikola Tesla, Josiah Royce, Josephine MacLeod, Betty Leggett, Emma Calvé, and Hermann Ludwig Ferdinand von Helmholtz.

With time, Swami Vivekananda started focusing more on establishing centres of Vedanta philosophy in the West. He focused on adapting the ideas of Hinduism to the understanding of the audience in the West, who had already gained familiarity with Western esoteric traditions of Transcendentalism and New Thought. He also introduced the "four yogas" model, which was his interpretation of *yoga sutras* by Patanjali. In 1896, he wrote a book called *Raja Yoga*, which went on to become a huge success in the Western understanding of yoga.

Soon, Swami Vivekananda felt the calling to build a monastery in the Himalayas as well as centres in Calcutta and Madras, Allahabad and Bombay. He expressed this it in a letter addressed to one of his disciples in 1896. During this time, he was also pleased that his magazine *Brahmavadin* – which was published from Madras – was doing well in terms of disseminating his thoughts and ideas. He also desired a paper to take his ideas to every part of the world. Above all, he felt a deep longing to return to India. And so, he started planning for his return to the country.

Teachings and Philosophy

Swami Vivekananda's core teachings rested on morality in terms of controlling the mind, the importance of seeing the Truth, mastering unselfish behaviour, and practising purity of the mind, body and soul. Towards this end, he advocated *brahmacharya* to his disciples to develop physical, mental, and emotional stamina.

His initial spiritual thoughts were shaped by his association with Brahmo Samaj, which believed in rejecting idol worship and believed in a God without any form. This was combined by a modernistic interpretation of the Upanishads and Vedanta philosophy. His early thought rested on the idea of the Divine existing in one all, irrespective of one's caste or social status. He believed in promoting love and harmony in society. His thoughts were further moulded by his association with Keshab Chandra Sen's *Nava Vidhan*, the Freemasonry lodge, and Band of Hope. During his travels to the West, he acquainted himself with Western esotericism.

The biggest influence, however, on Swami Vivekananda was that of Shri Ramakrishna, whose teachings led him to find his true inner self. Shri Ramakrishna introduced him to a Vedanta-worldview, which was simply the practice of looking at human beings as manifestations of the Divine Being. This led Swami Vivekananda to propagate his thoughts about Hinduism through Advaita Vedanta philosophy. Notwithstanding his belief in Advaita Vedanta, he believed the Absolute Divine to be immanent as well as transcendent. He sums it up as follows:

"Each soul is potentially divine. The goal is to manifest this Divinity within by controlling nature, external and internal. Do this either by work, or worship, or mental discipline, or philosophy—by one, or more, or all of these—and be free. This is the whole of religion."

His teachings were a synthesis of various groups of Hindu thoughts, notably Advaita Vedanta and classical yoga. Swami Vivekananda also laid emphasis on the concept of "involution", which he borrowed from the doctrines of Western Theosophy, as well as the concept of Evolution as theorised by Charles Darwin, and the Samkhya understanding of satkarya.

In terms of Western traditions in esotericism, Swami Vivekananda adapted his traditional teachings in Hinduism to suit the need and understanding of the people in the West. This made him one of the pioneering representatives of the Neo-Vedanta school of thought, which is a modern-day interpretation of Hinduism in congruence with the Western esoteric traditions of Transcendentalism, Theosophy, and

New Thought. This enabled him to strike a chord with this Western audiences, who, in turn, developed a deep appreciation for Hinduism as well as for the practice of yoga, transcendental meditation and other methods of getting in touch with the spiritual self. Although deemed as reductionist in view, his ultimate though was that irrespective of the differences among the various sects in Hinduism, they all espoused different paths to reach the same goal.

Finally, the concept of nationalism was an integral part of Swami Vivekananda's thoughts. He placed people at the centre of a country's future and emphasised on holistic human development towards this end.

The Legacy of Swami Vivekananda

On 16th December 1896, Swami Vivekananda and his disciples Captain and Mrs. Sevier, as well as J.J. Goodwin, left for India from England. Their ship made stopovers in France and Italy as they made their way towards India. On 15th January 1897, the ship reached the shores of Colombo, in Ceylon (now known as Sri Lanka). Their group was greeted by notable people in Colombo, who not only sang religious hymns but also sprinkled rose water on the group. Visitors also made offerings of fruit and flowers to them. Later, Swami Vivekananda addressed the visitors in his first public speech in Ceylon.

From Colombo, he and his disciples journeyed to Madras where the Raja of Ramnad – who encouraged the Swami to visit the United States welcomed him back. From here, wherever Swami Vivekananda would travel in India, he was met with a grand reception by his ever-growing following who would try to catch a glimpse of the spiritual master

People welcoming Swami Vivekananda

one way or another. In Rameshwaram, the Raja installed a victory column in honour of Swami Vivekananda to mark his homecoming.

As Swami Vivekananda travelled from Madras to Calcutta and further to Almora, he made public speeches not just focusing on the spiritual heritage of India, but also on the prevailing social issues, such as the caste system, upliftment of people, alleviating poverty, industrialisation, the need for inculcating a scientific temper, and ending the British Colonial rule. Many of these lectures are compiled in a book called *Lectures from Colombo to Almora*.

Final Years of Swami Vivekananda

In 1897, Swami Vivekananda established the Ramakrishna Mission in Calcutta. A profound commitment to serve humankind was at the heart of the Ramakrishna Mission's formation. Through the Ramakrishna Mission, Swami Vivekananda sought to disseminate the teachings of Ramakrishna Paramhansa and foster spiritual growth among individuals of diverse faiths. In his pursuit of this mission, Swami Vivekananda championed the education of followers in spiritual sciences, encouraged participation in industry and the arts, and disseminated the principles of Vedanta philosophy. The Ramakrishna Mission had two distinct departments, each responsible for overseeing the organization's operations within India and internationally.

In conjunction with the Ramakrishna Mission, the Ramakrishna Math was to conduct the religious work. Today, both the organisations have their headquarters in Belur Math, near present-day Kolkata, in West Bengal. In following his long-cherished dream of setting up a monastery in the Himalayas, Swami Vivekananda founded one in Mayavati, near Almora, as well as the Advaita Ashram in Madras. In addition, he launched two journals: *Prabuddha Bharata* in English and *Udbhodan* in Bangla.

Swami Vivekananda and Jamsetji Tata

In 1893, when Jamsetji Tata and Swami Vivekananda travelled together from Yokohama to Chicago during Vivekananda's first trip to the West, Vivekananda encouraged Jamsetji Tata to create a research and educational institution. Later, Swami Vivekananda denied Tata's offer to lead his Research Institute of Science, claiming it would clash with his "spiritual objectives".

By 1899, Swami Vivekananda's health had begun to decline. All these years of being a wandering monk, working long hours, extensive travel, and life in harsh conditions had started to tell on his physical well-being. Despite physical ailments, Swami Vivekananda decided to again travel to the West in June the same year. Sister Nivedita and Swami Turiyananda were in attendance with him. During this visit, he established Vedanta Societies in New York and San Francisco. He also established a peace retreat in California. From here, Swami Vivekananda went on to represent India at the Congress of Religions, in Paris, in 1900. Then, he visited Brittany, Vienna, Athens, Istanbul, and Egypt.

Swami Vivekanand's visit to Istanbul

When he returned to India, he learnt about the death of his disciple, Mr. Sevier, in Mayavati. This brought him so much grief that he immediately prepared for his journey to Mayavati to meet his wife, Mrs. Sevier. After an emotional meeting where he paid his condolences, he returned to Belur Math and continued with the work of coordinating the spiritual activities of Ramakrishna Mission, as well the work of the spiritual societies and centres in the US and UK. However, his health had begun to worsen as he struggled with diabetes, asthma, and chronic insomnia. As a result, he couldn't attend the Congress of Religions, in Japan, in 1901.

Death of Swami Vivekananda

Swami Vivekananda spent his last years in Belur Math, leading a wholesome life, which comprised roaming around the grounds, supervising the monastery kitchen, cooking food for his disciples, and joining his followers to sing devotional songs. Even though his health was deteriorating, he kept going about his day-to-day life in the monastery, rarely taking rest. Even in 1901, Swami Vivekananda observed all the festivals that year at Belur Math. On Durga Puja, a huge feast was cooked for the city's poor. In February, the following year, large-scale preparations were made at Belur Math to celebrate the birth anniversary of Shri Ramakrishna – it is said more than 30,000 devotees attended the celebration. Swami Vivekananda couldn't join the festivities for he was unwell but watched the fervent celebrations from a window in his room.

31 Ailments of Swami Vivekananda

According to renowned Bengali author, Shankar, Swami Vivekananda had 31 health issues during his lifetime. These included insomnia, liver and renal disorders, malaria, migraines, diabetes, and heart conditions among them.

But on the fateful day of 4th July 1902, the inevitable happened. On this day, Swami Vivekananda woke up early and meditated for nearly three hours in the monastery. He taught his students and even discussed with his colleagues the opening of a Vedic college in Ramakrishna Math. By evening, he checked into his room and asked not to be disturbed. He sat down to meditate and continued to be in that state for the next three hours. He died at 9.20 pm while in a meditative state.

Immediately, the people at the monastery called in physicians who tried artificial respiration. By midnight, it was confirmed that Swami Vivekananda had departed the world. His disciples believe Swami Vivekananda attained the state of *mahasamadhi* (a state of meditative consciousness) and that led to a blood vessel to burst in his brain. The official reason of his demise was apoplexy or heart failure. With this, Swami Vivekananda had, in fact, fulfilled his prophecy years ago when he declared that he won't live beyond 40 years. The next morning his followers poured in from all corners of the country. Sister Nivedita sat by his body and fanned it till he was brought to the courtyard. His cremation took place in Belur along the banks of the Ganges where Shri Ramakrishna was cremated 16 years before.

An Enduring Legacy

Mahatma Gandhi described him as one of the reformers "who have maintained this Hindu religion in a state of splendour by cutting down the dead wood of tradition". Swami Vivekananda left a legacy of spiritualism that has endured the test of time and has come to align with the values of modern-day Indians. In 2010, the late Pranab Mukherjee, the then Finance Minister, approved the Swami Vivekananda Values Education Project, worth ₹1 billion, which aims to involve the youth in discussions, competitions, and study circles, as well as publishing the works of Swami Vivekananda in various languages.

Additionally, in 2011, the West Bengal Police Training College was rechristened as Swami Vivekananda Police Academy. In 2012, the airport in Ranchi was also renamed as Swami Vivekananda Airport. Today, the life of Swami Vivekananda is commemorated on his birthday, 12th January, which has been declared as National Youth Day. Moreover, the day that he made his landmark speech at the Parliament of Religions on 11th September 1893 is observed as World Brotherhood Day. More recently, in 2013, the 150th birthday of Swami Vivekananda was celebrated with great pomp and show in India and overseas.

8

Notable Achievements

Swami Vivekananda dedicated his life to his Mission, both within India and outside of the country. At the core, he wanted to serve mankind as well as promote peace and brotherhood. He embraced the Vedanta philosophy and based his thoughts and actions on the tenets of it. All along he was hyperaware of the physical reality surrounding him as well as the spiritual divinity within.

Over his fairly short life span of 39 years, Swami Vivekananda exercised deep mindfulness for the service of mankind while struggling with declining health. He spent much of the latter half of his life travelling within India as well as to the countries of the West. During these years, he delivered public addresses, lectures, composed poems, founded Vedanta societies in the West, and gave spiritual guidance to countless people. Above all, he founded the Ramakrishna Math, which is one of the paramount religious organisations in contemporary India to this day.

As a monk, philosopher, religious teacher, and an author, Swami Vivekananda made significant achievements in various spheres, of which the significant ones are mentioned here:

1. Swami Vivekananda revitalised modern Hinduism and advance nationalist consciousness during the Colonia era.

2. Ramakrishna Ashram was founded by Swami Vivekananda in 1897. In 1899, he founded the Belur Math on the west bank of the Ganges.

3. Swami Vivekananda's works on Hindu philosophy and Vedanta principles include *Jnana-Yoga, Bhakti-Yoga, Karma-Yoga*, and *Raja-Yoga*.

4. Swami Vivekananda was referred to as "the Maker of Modern India" by notable freedom fighter, Subhas Chandra Bose.

5. His lecture at the Parliament of Religions in Chicago, in 1893, led to the introduction of the tenets of Hinduism to the West and went on to establish him as a leading spiritual figure in world.

6. On 12th January, India celebrates National Youth Day in remembrance of Swami Vivekananda's ideals on how young people should interact with the modern world.

7. In March 1899, Swami Vivekananda wrote *Bartaman Bharat* (Present-Day India) which was a scholarly essay in Bengali language. It was published in *Udbhodhan*, a Bengali magazine of Ramakrishna Mission and Ramakrishna Math. It was printed as a book in 1905.

8. Some of the notable books that were published during his lifetime were *Sangeet Kalpataru* (1887), *Vedanta Philosophy: An address before the Graduate Philosophical Society* (1896), and *Lectures from Colombo to Almora* (1897).

9. His works *The East and the West* (1909), *Inspired Talks* (1909), *Practical Vedanta, Seeing Beyond the Circle* (2005).

9

Swami Vivekananda's Famous Quotes

Here are a few inspiring quotes by Swami Vivekananda that reflect his indomitable spirit and dedication towards his life purpose:

- "Arise! Awake! and stop not until the goal is reached."
- "We are what our thoughts have made us; so take care about what you think. Words are secondary. Thoughts live; they travel far."
- "Where can we go to find God if we cannot see Him in our own hearts and in every living being."
- "Take up one idea. Make that one idea your life – think of it, dream of it, live on that idea. Let the brain, muscles, nerves, every part of your body, be full of that idea, and just leave every other idea alone. This is the way to success."
- "You cannot believe in God until you believe in yourself."
- "The whole secret of existence is to have no fear. Never fear what will become of you, depend on no one. Only the moment you reject all help are you freed."
- "Truth can be stated in a thousand different ways, yet each one can be true."

- "All differences in this world are of degree, and not of kind, because oneness is the secret of everything."

- "Condemn none: if you can stretch out a helping hand, do so. If you cannot, fold your hands, bless your brothers, and let them go their own way."

- "The moment I have realized God sitting in the temple of every human body, the moment I stand in reverence before every human being and see God in him – that moment I am free from bondage, everything that binds vanishes, and I am free."

- "When an idea exclusively occupies the mind, it is transformed into an actual physical or mental state."

- "The Vedanta recognizes no sin it only recognizes error. And the greatest error, says the Vedanta is to say that you are weak, that you are a sinner, a miserable creature, and that you have no power and you cannot do this and that."

- "If money help a man to do good to others, it is of some value; but if not, it is simply a mass of evil, and the sooner it is got rid of, the better."

- "The will is not free – it is a phenomenon bound by cause and effect – but there is something behind the will which is free."

Learning from Swami Vivekananda's Life

Swami Vivekananda's life has served as an inspiration to countless women and men in finding their sense of self and higher path in life. Hence, it is no surprise that his birth anniversary has been declared as National Youth Day. In contemporary India, Swami Vivekananda is considered a youth icon for following the path to spiritual enrichment, teaching equanimity and humanity, and showing the way to scores of people who sought spiritual guidance from him. Even today, he continues to inspire generations of people with life lessons and an understanding of ways in which these spiritual goals can be reached.

Poster for National Youth Day published by the Government of India, celebrated on January 12, birth anniversary of Swami Vivekananda

Swami Vivekananda is revered as the patron saint of modern India's patriotism and an inspiration to the country's national consciousness. Throughout his life, he preached the tenets of the philosophy of Hinduism as one that is centred on giving strength to its followers and disciples. One of his biggest lessons to followers of Hinduism was to shift their focus from rituals and ancient myths to becoming humanitarian and serving for the good of others. These ideals have long inspired a line of political leaders of country in leading the path towards independence from the Colonial masters.

Swami Vivekananda dedicated his life to his mission of promoting peace and brotherhood – which was the foundational truth of Vedanta philosophy – not just in India but overseas as well. His life was always a precarious balance of seeking the path towards realising the Highest Truth as well as being present in the material world and working towards the alleviation of human suffering. All along, one would have thought that he was walking a tightrope between serving his mission in this world and answering his Higher calling.

Wherever the path to salvation took him, Swami Vivekananda carried a part of his country with himself. He often referred to himself as "a condensed India". As a pioneer of Vedanta philosophy in the West, he captured the imagination of not just eminent philosophers and scientists of the time, but also of the public at large. Famous Harvard University philosopher, William James, used to call him "the paragon of Vedantists".

Swami Vivekananda's teachings continue to inspire people across the world to this day. Even today, Ramakrishna Mission and Ramakrishna Math serve as great centres of spiritual learning, guiding the lives of its followers and showing the road to finding one's Higher calling in life and, above all, being of service to mankind.

www.ingramcontent.com/pod-product-compliance
Lightning Source LLC
LaVergne TN
LVHW092032190726
843493LV00002B/658